LIMINAL HOUSE / MCLEOD BOVELL

MASTERPIECE
SERIES

LIMINAL HOUSE / MCLEOD BOVELL
INTRODUCTION BY AARON BETSKY | ESSAY BY BOTANICA DESIGN
PRINCIPAL PHOTOGRAPHY BY HUFTON + CROW | EDITED BY OSCAR RIERA OJEDA

OSCAR RIERA OJEDA
PUBLISHERS

# CONTENTS

| | |
|---|---|
| INTRODUCTION | 010 |
| BY AARON BETSKY | |
| | |
| DESIGN | 016 |
| DESCRIPTION | 018 |
| PRESENTATION DRAWINGS | 020 |
| | |
| CONSTRUCTION | 032 |
| WORKING DRAWINGS | 034 |
| PROCESS | 048 |
| | |
| BUILDING | 074 |
| | |
| LANDSCAPE | 148 |
| ESSAY BY BOTANICA DESIGN | 150 |
| DETAILS | 152 |
| | |
| APPENDIX | 184 |
| PROJECT CREDITS | 186 |
| PHOTOGRAPHY CAPTIONS | 188 |
| DESIGNERS | 196 |
| BOOK CREDITS | 200 |

# INTRODUCTION
## BY AARON BETSKY

**A Loft With a View:**
**McLeod Bovell's Liminal House**

Views tend to swallow up those houses that have them. That is the challenge designers face when offered the opportunity to imagine a home on a site with a spectacular prospect. Not only do such vistas tend to overwhelm the interior from which one takes them in but obtaining the most of that asset means suppressing every other aspect of the design. Moreover, the site for such view homes is usually one of contest, with all the neighbours vying for the same angle and the necessity of servicing the actual operation of the buildings continually conflicting with that aim. In the so-called Liminal House, by Canadian designers Matthew McLeod and Lisa Bovell in West Vancouver, that struggle is not so much overcome, as made into a composition of glorious moments in and around one central loft.

Mcleod Bovell is specialized in designing for such situations. A small firm based in downtown Vancouver, they have developed, as they themselves say, a "niche market" that depends on word-of-mouth and drive-bys of completed projects. Most of those commissions are in West Vancouver, the area across the Burrard Inlet and below the North Shore Mountains that looks back to the downtown area and out towards the Strait of Georgia and its many islands and ships. In the dozen years that the firm has been in operation, it has completed over forty projects in this situation.

All of these structures use the same minimalist approach. The designers make them out of concrete, which they cover partially on the outside with either treated timber or tile that evoke that material. On the inside, they also use woods that they gather into sheets that act as screens or partial flooring, ceilings, or walls, while always allowing the concrete cocoon to remain dominant. The windows to the view side are large, usually floor-to-ceiling and often designed to retract to let the space flow between inside and outside. Within this framework, the designers break down the overall volume, when they have enough room, to create interior courtyards. This both balances the light from the front and provides focal points and viewing gardens for those rooms that do not have access to that expanse. Staircases and light wells connect and open the spaces further on the often steeply sloping and narrow sites that necessitate several levels of living area. The detailing of all these forms and materials is exquisite in its ability to hide or discipline into minimalist punctuations whatever is needed to make the projects come together. "We wanted the result to be a "something," as opposed to the "nothing" we see all around us," comments Bovell.

The firm has developed their method, according to the principals, not so much as a continuation of the traditions of the

AARON BETSKY is a critic living in Philadelphia. Previously, he was Director of the School of Architecture and Design at Virginia Tech and President of the School of Architecture at Taliesin. Mr. Betsky is the author of over twenty books on those subjects. He writes a once-weekly blog for architectmagazine.com, Beyond Buildings. Trained as an architect and in the humanities at Yale University, Mr. Betsky has served as the Director of the Cincinnati Art Museum (2006-2014) and the Netherlands Architecture Institute (2001-2006), as well as Curator of Architecture and Design at the San Francisco Museum of Modern Art (1995-2001). In 2008, he also directed the 11th Venice International Biennale of Architecture. His latest books are *Fifty Lessons from Frank Lloyd Wright* (2021), *Making It Modern* (2019), *Architecture Matters* (2019) and *Anarchitecture: The Monster Leviathan*.

area's architecture, as out of a combination of learning from contemporary work on an international level and practical experience. The former is the result of their assessment of the low quality of most of the work around them and the lack of what they see as an appropriate tradition of building, especially among homes in Vancouver. Though they do reach back to the early work of Arthur Erickson and Ron Thom, as well as to their teacher at the University of British Columbia, Patricia Patkau, they see that design as having remained isolated. Rather, the expressive minimalism they see in Southern California (especially in the work of John Lautner) and Europe serves them as inspiration. This sense of building in an international mode also echoes their clientele, most of whom are relatively recent arrivals from Europe, Asia, and Australia.

The design work McLeod Bovell have developed in this situation is about control. It is about both disciplining and exploiting the view and the site, screening out as much as possible the messiness of roads, train tracks, power lines, and, above all else, ugly neighbours, while also making sure the free expanse the home overlooks does not completely swallow them up. It is also the result of a minimalist approach that frees the clients to enjoy their expensive sliver of real estate as much as possible and making the forms not so much go away, as behave. If there's sculptural moments in their designs, and there are many, they are composed to either emphasize the progression towards the view or to organize, without separating, different living areas. The control even continues to the way the firm works. Eschewing some of the more sophisticated software and CAD other designers employ, they use simpler tools like Sketch Up to communicate easily with each other, clients, and builders. They even work hard to ensure that all the monitors that march down the desks of their narrow studio are exactly the same model.

The Liminal House is the design in which many of the aspects of these designers' practice come together in the most sophisticated manner. Partially this is the result of the desires and internal discipline (and the means) of their clients. A family of two adults with three sons, they wanted something "grand" and yet practical. They also wanted to have a true home where they could come together.

The combination of coziness and grandeur was especially important to them, as they also realized that, with their sons all approaching college age, the parents would soon be empty nesters. One last particularity to their program of one principal and three children's bedrooms, an expansive living area, and such ancillary spaces as a study, a gym, and a home theatre, was the need for a place for them to store as many of the cars the husband collects as possible.

Because of the nature of the site's steep slope and local building regulations limiting height, McLeod Bovell placed the main living area about eight meters below the access road to the rear. A steep driveway slopes and angles past a rear court used by the boys for sports and to a covered entrance. Once alighted, you enter by navigating past a light well that brings illumination to both this and the lower level. You immediately see the view, but it is partially obscured by a box covered in white oak that is the space's main service core. The opening of the scissored stair to your right, which also brings light into the middle of the lot here, and a much larger interior court that terminates at this level, directs you towards the main living area. It is there that the full expanse of the both the Great Room, as it would have been called in an English manor house, and the view across the Strait and Inlet fully opens.

That openness seems natural at first, until you realize that it is made possible, as with most of these designers' work, by extensive structural gymnastics that are hidden in the depth of the smoothly finished concrete ceiling. To create the full span, the plane above you is at points more than a meter deep. This also brings it somewhat lower in front of the floor-to-ceiling windows, which slide to one side in good weather, further emphasizing the horizontal sweep of what you are confronted with in this excavation of the site. A small swimming pool in front of the house brings the water close to the living areas.

This main space serves much the same function of a loft, and has some of the industrial, or at least rough and minimalist, qualities of such converted industrial spaces. Though both horizontal and vertical planes are broken up into areas of wood, white stucco, a sintered stone called Lapitec, and poured concrete, the overwhelming sense is of being in a box carved out of a much later structure – even if that is a natural (stone), rather than a human-made one. "We wanted to make a place that would collect the house's activity," says McLeod. "That is a strategy we use in general," adds Bovell, "rather than making separate rooms that suck people towards them, we want to bring as much together as possible." It seems to work: "This is where we spend all of our time," says the client. "It has that great sense of space, but I feel completely cozy here."

The only separate elements within this loft are the kitchen island, which acts as a magnet for the family and a place of work when meals are being prepared, and the wood box. This object, which Mcleod Bovell have used in other houses as well, becomes a sink for all that is necessary, but unseemly, for the loft to operate: storage, a hall closet and guest bathroom, and an elevator. It also serves a major structural role. One small part of the loft leaks out beyond all this: a small study at the rear end of the kitchen area for one of the clients. From here, she can see the comings and goings along the driveway, while also being sheltered from the activities in the living area.

Above the loft is a second expansive space. This is the principal bedroom, which takes up the complete front of the house as well. The bedroom and bathroom area are separated from each other by an extension of the wood box below and can only be partially shut off from each other. The walk-in closet then takes up the area directly behind this front room.

This means that none of the other three bedrooms have any part of the view. This is perhaps the most radical aspect of the Liminal House. In its clear focus on bringing people together in the front areas, it relegates the rooms for the boys to a row in which they share a view of a rock garden that rambles along the side of the house on this level and a concrete wall beyond. Though receiving ample light, the rooms take the designers' (and clients') minimalism to an extreme, creating the kind of meditative and secluded set of environments more common to some modern Japanese houses.

The lower level is the depository for the other spaces the house needed. The core extends to this floor and around it McLeod Bovell organized a den, a spa, a gym, and an office. Only the office has a view, while the other rooms receive light from the light wells. To the rear is another kind of loft, this one large enough to house up to six cars, which is reached by an elevator from the main garage above.

The Liminal House is visible as an object only from the beach and the Inlet beyond. It presents itself as concrete walls and balustrades jutting forward towards that larger environment at acute angles and between continuous bands of glass. You would never know how the house rambles back to the rear of the long lot. As on the interior, the house presents itself only to the view.

What makes the home come together, even more so than in previous houses McLeod Bovell has completed, is the way it is assembled. There are barely any reveals, and certainly no ornamentation or even elements such as base boards or lintels to mask any of the construction. Every plane is brought together as if by magic, sometimes to a degree that it makes you wonder what structural gymnastics – miniature versions of the main ones that make the spaces possible – are going on inside those walls. Where planes are articulated, they are brought into complete harmony with each other: the vertical oak boards on the stair railings line up perfectly with the treads and risers. "The client held us to the same level of craftsmanship and engineering as he expects from his Ferraris," explains McLeod, who is himself a vintage performance car enthusiast.

The designers compare the Liminal House to some of the sea creatures that live on and near the adjacent beach in their protective carapaces. Within its protective exterior it shelters a set of seemingly simple, but finely honed spaces. Unlike these animals, however, this house is engineered not for one being, but for a family to come together, work, and grow. It also marks itself as resolutely made by human beings who delight in their ability to capture at least a part of the epic grandeur of Vancouver's nature, domesticate it, and make themselves at home within that larger space. At the edge between urban life and nature, McLeod Bovell have made the ultimate loft with a view.

DESIGN

# DESCRIPTION

Our work embraces social, spatial and environmental opportunities as catalysts for invention. We balance the demands of natural prospects with the advantages afforded by challenging topography to generate varied and particular programmatic sequences. The studio prioritizes an integrative design approach in which every project is imagined and created comprehensively. For this reason, interior and hard landscape design are developed simultaneously in-house as part of a complete design process. We have fostered close collaborations with local designers and consultants to generate specific strategies that align with our conceptualization of the project and we use modelling as a tool to refine complex spatial and material intersections.

The site for this project is located on rugged terrain at the base of the North Shore Mountains in West Vancouver, British Columbia, in Western Canada. This stretch of coastline, bounded by Burrard Inlet to the south and Howe Sound to the west, is desirable for its broad vistas southward towards the city of Vancouver and westward towards the Gulf Islands. Although this territory exists conceptually within an extravagant natural world, the ground is neither untouched wilderness nor fully cultivated landscape. Rather, it exists a bit strangely at the intersection of the waterfront and a suburban residential neighbourhood. The clients for the Liminal House came to us as soon-to-be "empty nesters" with their domestic and professional lives in transition. We imagined the patterns of our client's occupation of the house as tidal movements advancing and retreating from an extended shoreline.

To address these many complex relationships, sequences within the house are primarily understood as a series of continuously unfolding dynamic experiences. Conventionally static, two-dimensional viewpoints are suppressed by circumstance and intention. An emphasis on movement is intertwined with a deliberate deployment of refractive strategies in order to generate a kind of benign disorientation of the eye and body. We realized that efforts to disrupt normalizing psychological processes would allow the house to acquire a deeper, more engaging life for its inhabitants. Movement is choreographed by ramping and stepping through an interconnected series of garden courtyards and light wells located roughly along the centre of the site. Materials were specified in an effort to balance the impermeable with the porous; concrete and glass. Like the creatures that dwell along the rocky shore, the house exhibits adaptations that aid it in withstanding external kinetic forces while simultaneously allowing perfusion through a soft internal body.

At the ever changing border of land and sea, the house is charged with a series of tasks and becomes the mediator between a variety of significant forces: the demands of the view, the physical requirements of construction on a site that sits within a compressed suburban context and the requirement to adapt to the changing needs of a family over time. These realities converged to create an idea for a house that could exist in an inbetween or "liminal" state. Etymologically, the latin term "limen" refers to a threshold. It is a transitional moment between where something begins and another ends; where differing elements meet, mix, and merge. Imagining the project within this framework allowed us to employ strategies that we hoped would have the potential to authentically connect the narrative of the design directly to the received qualities of the building. Conceptually, the house became a constructed shoreline between water and land where various agendas are resolved through a vocabulary that is both hard and tough while simultaneously soft and open, excavated yet still expansive.

# PRESENTATION DRAWINGS

Regional Map

Upper Floor Plan
1. Upper Garden | 2. Guest Suite Terrace | 3. Lightwell to Autocourt | 4. Guest Suite | 5. Bedroom W/Ensuite | 6. Bedroom W/Ensuite
7. Lightwell to Basement | 8. Principal Bedroom | 9. Principal Ensuite | 10. Walk in Closet

Main Floor Plan
1. Autocourt | 2. Garage | 3. Mudroom | 4. Washroom / Laundry | 5. Coutyard Garden | 6. Entry | 7. Lightwell to Basement | 8. Desk
9. Kitchen / Dining | 10. Living Room | 11. Powder Room | 12. Covered Terrace | 13. Pool

Basement Floor Plan
1. Car Storage | 2. Office | 3. Recreation Room | 4. Laundry Room | 5. Spa Bathroom / Sauna | 6. Guest Bedroom |
7. Lightwell to Basement | 8. Covered Terrace | 9. Pool Storage | 10. Spa | 11. Beach Stairs | 12. Lower Garden | 13. Pool Stairs

Context Plan

South Elevation

North Elevation

East Elevation

Short Section

Long Section 01

# CONSTRUCTION

# WORKING DRAWINGS

Main floor concrete slab plan

Main floor concrete wall plan

Upper floor concrete plan

Upper floor

Main floor

Basement floor

Living / Dining details

Living / Dining details

Lightwell / Stairwell details

044 | CONSTRUCTION / WORKING DRAWINGS

Lightwell / Stairwell details

Garage / Mudroom details

Garage / Mudroom details

# PROCESS

BUILDING

LANDSCAPE

# ESSAY
## BY BOTANICA DESIGN

**CONTEXT**

This project is a paradox, and is in many ways a landscape of extremes. The location exists at the threshold of a variety of disparate elements: sunny and shady, breezy and stagnant, up in the air and at sea level, public and private, mountainside and seaside.

We were influenced by the dynamic natural landscapes that existed in the immediate vicinity. Our observations of local seaside meadows led to a carefully curated seaside plant palette with a scrubby, sparse, informal appearance. Plantings that grow in close proximity to the ocean tend to be stunted due to the harsh, tough growing conditions with foliage that is frequently silver-hued and hairy to protect from the extremes of light, temperature and wind. Thicker leaves are also typical as they are adapted to episodes of drought. The use of grasses to provide a substructure for the garden physically support a scattering of taller, less stable perennials. Grasses that would typically thrive at the seaside can have a tendency to spread and invade so, though it limited plant choice, a clumping Festuca was selected which behaves respectfully toward other species.

The south side of the property is exposed to ocean elements and may be hot or cold and breezy with saline air. Collaborating closely with a local grower / plantsman, we developed a sun-loving plant combination that would contribute to a durable seaside garden and thrive in a harsh environment.

We selected native and "native-like" plant material for the larger framework for the garden. We were able to incorporate complexity through texture in the higher canopy by sourcing coniferous (Pinus), broadleaf evergreen (Myrica) and deciduous (Salix) shrubs to create layers and also reflect local natural mountainous surroundings.

The idea of a seaside meadow was stretched through the site, weaving around the pool and up to the upper floor roof-top planting and from the waterfront to the garden at the street. A planted green roof was constructed at the upper level. This manufactured condition presented obstacles, including sourcing a specific lightweight soil medium that would satisfy the maximum roof loading requirements. In certain areas, the soil depth was significantly restricted. Lightweight plant bags were sourced to accommodate plant shrubs with larger root bases. Hippophae was selected because it thrives in well draining soil medium within the fibrous material of the soft bag and because it withstands exposure to sea air.

There were also challenges of deep shade and air stagnation resulting from north facing gardens, overhanging building conditions and deep light wells which, though dramatic, required plant editing due to difficult growing conditions. In these areas, plants that were acclimatized to the understory of a forest were selected and had to endure similar stresses that would occur in a natural forest habitat where only the most robust species endure.

The hardscape elements can be divided into two categories, those associated with the house and those which have a stronger relationship to the local landscape. Hardscape materials adjacent to the house are formal and clean, comprised primarily of concrete, sintered stone and black aluminum plate. These materials were used in retaining walls, at the pool perimeters, at the covered terrace, and at the cobbled auto court. Alternatively, structural materials that were located within the zone of the planted landscape were chosen for their organic shapes and irregularly shaped rough-sawn faces. Black basalt was sourced from a local quarry. The flexibility provided by irregularly shaped steps allowed for nuanced adjustments to complex topography. Heavy aggregate was introduced in areas of the property as a ground treatment transition between the home and the garden beyond.

A variety of basalt rock in different thicknesses and in different forms was utilized to create stepping stone paths and patios, staircase treads, aggregate and large boulders. This material was used to facilitate access and interaction with the planting to provide the experience of being immersed in the garden rather than a simple visual experience.

BOTANICA DESIGN is a landscape design/build studio founded in 1998 and located in Vancouver, British Columbia. We are a collaborative team of designers, builders and horticulturists dedicated to creating, constructing and maintaining thoughtful and well built landscapes. With a shared approach, our gardens are realized utilizing both theoretical and practical knowledge. Through a process of inquiry, our work is continuously evolving. Although we are largely a creative studio, we are practical beyond belief and considerate of all aspects of the project. Maintenance plays an integral role in the formation of our intended vision. Our belief is that the best designs are built over time by knowledgable, skilled and creative gardeners. As both designers and constructors we are able to merge all facets of a project to create a seamless design-build process that leaves nothing lost in translation.

## MOOD and ATMOSPHERE

The hard, often dark exterior of the house is enduring like the exoskeleton of a crustacean. The landscape weaving through it and around it is, at times, bright and ephemeral.

Ornamental grasses and perennials were selected with the intention of expressing movement and capturing light. These plant traits are instrumental in developing an effortless mood in a garden. The seed heads of Stipa calamagrostis are illuminated by the sunset reflected in the ocean. The plants within the meadow intermingle and change daily, highlighting the feeling of life and impermanence: ebb and flow.

While light and kinetic movement play an integral role in shaping the atmosphere of the gardens, these strategies predominate in the brighter, uncovered, open spaces on the periphery of the house. In contrast, covered cave-like pockets created by the shape of the house (courtyards, light wells, overhangs) are dark and cinematic. Plantings in these zones may intentionally appear rigid and static, presenting darker hues with strong textures and legible leaf shapes – a kind of dream underworld that is refracted and reflected through the house's internally glazed spaces.

Movement through the garden is emotive and creates a sensory experience. Birds socialize and scavenge while the scent from the garden drifts through the ocean air. Blooms intermingle with bending grasses inviting you to physically experience the textures at hand.

## SEASONALITY

A garden is an evolving, living process. The plants chosen for Liminal House included conifers, deciduous trees, shrubs, perennials, grasses and ground-covers. Layering plant material and choosing a multitude of plant species establishes a palette with continuity of visual interest that is also attractive to a biodiverse community of animal species. We refer to this ever-changing presentation as a symphony, referencing its structure, tone and rhythmic shifts. When one plant is in season, others are present only in the background, supporting the narrative, but not sharing the limelight. Every plant has a task and a moment.

We admire every component of a plant's life cycle. For perennials and bulbs this is a birth, death and a rebirth. Gardens should be fully captivating to all senses and provide a benefit to the living species around them throughout the entire year – for shelter and food. We select plants that are notable for scent, structure, seed heads, movement, fall colour and foliage. When the timing of these attributes avoids competition amongst the plants, we have succeeded.

Bloom sequence and flower shape in a garden creates compositional diversity. The soil erupts with bulbs in early Spring and the symphony continues into the early summer months. An enormous variety of naturalizing and hybrid Tulips are paired with Narcissus, Anemone, Frittilaria, etc. to create a carpet of colour, breaking winter dormancy.

Summer is the peak season. The plants are bright, vigorous and abundant. Brilliant hued blooms are teeming with pollinators and the air vibrates with life. There is a slight shift in the tone of the foliage between summer and early fall when ornamental grasses develop seed heads and foliage starts to bleach. Autumn makes a gentle appearance in this garden with nuance. The one exception are the soaring Fagus hedgerows flanking the east and west side of the property whose leaves turn dramatic shades of yellow and copper.

The winter season brings decay but the plant structure remains engaging, particularly when touched by frost. As this seasonal shift happens and the florets transform into seeds, they become a food source for birds which enhances the allure and energy within the garden. The entire composition is considered together and it is our hope that all the senses are impacted by these experiences. The passage of time, stages of life, and specific species are recognized and celebrated.

# DETAILS

Lower Garden Hardscape

B - Boulder (Typical) - Black Basalt

Patio Stone - Sawn basalt w/natural edge. 2" Thick. Flamed top. Dry set on crushed limestone base. Bedrock Stone Supply - Black Basalt

Stone Walkways/Staircase - Sawn w/flamed top. Natural edge. Average dimension 2'x3'. All treads to be 6" thick. Dry set on compacted base material (roadbase).

Aggregate Rock (Typical) - 2-6" Black Basalt Murin Construction
Min depth of 4" required.
Landscape fabric under all aggregate

Irrigation:
Provide irrigation to all plant material
Total of (10) zones:
    Zone 1-3 - Drip lines for all hedging (Y,Z,j)
    Zone 4 - Drip irrigation to all Trees
    Zone 5-7 - In ground plant material zones (pop up spray heads)
      5 - Boulevard (North planting areas)
      6 - East side yard
      7 - South yard plantings
    Zone 8 - Lawn area
    Zone 9 - Courtyard Planting area (pop up spray heads)
    Zone 10 - Light well planting area (pop up spray heads)
System to comply with IIABC "Standard for Landscape Irrigation Systems"

Planter/Containers: (quantity = 1)

Bacsac - Geotextile circle raised 'Bacround 930 litres'
60" diameter

| Landscape Lighting | |
|---|---|
| Wall Wash Light "WAC Wall Wash LED, 12V" | 22 |
| Path Light "BK Lighting Lightstick". Aluminum Black, 18" | 4 |

NOTE - All Fixtures 2700K (warm white)
NOTE - Transformer/Timer located in Mechanical (Condenser) area

Lower Garden Softscape

## Roof Garden Hardscape

B - Boulder (Typical) - Black Basalt

Aggregate (Typical) - 3"-6" Black Basalt
Murin Construction
Min depth of 4" required.
Landscape fabric under all river rock areas

Planter/Containers: (quantity = 8)

Bacsac - Geotextile circle raised 'Bacround 930 litres'
60" (5) and 48" (3) diameter

Patio Stone - Sawn basalt w/natural edge. 3" Thick.
Flamed top. Dry set on crushed limestone base.
Bedrock Stone Supply - Black Basalt

R - Fire Place Feature - PALOFORM BOL 42' Corten
   250 pounds

Soil Depth - Min soil depth required 6". Bermed soil areas
to reach a max depth of 18" in some locations.

Drain Mat and landscape filter cloth required under all landscaped
areas over building structure.

Irrigation:
Provide irrigation to all plant material
Total of (3) zones:
   Zone 1 - in ground plant material - pop up spray heads
   Zone 2 - Drip irrigation to all planters
   Zone 3 - Drip (ring) irrigation for all trees
System to comply with IIABC "Standard for Landscape Irrigation Systems"

## Roof Garden Softscape

# APPENDIX

# PROJECT CREDITS

**Location**
West Vancouver, British Columbia, Canada

**Area**
10,940 square feet

**Project Construction**
2017 - 2022

**Designer**
Mcleod Bovell

**Design Team**
Lisa Bovell
Matthew Mcleod
Daan Murray
Daniel Ching

**Landscape Design**
Karin Hers-Schaffner
Otto Schaffner

**Client**
Private

**Building Photography**
Hufton & Crow

**Construction Photography**
Hart Tipton
Botanica Design

**Details Photography**
Matt McLeod

**Landscape Photography**
Britney Gill

**Civil Engineer**
Creus Engineering:
Fred Ciambrelli

**Geotechnical Engineer**
GVH Consulting Ltd.:
Greg Ven Huizen

**Envelope Engineer**
JRS Engineering Ltd.:
Ross Arbo
Adam Jarolim

**Structural Engineer**
Ennova Engineering:
Tim Lam

**Mechanical Engineer**
Ecolighten Energy Solutions:
Rob Pope

**Land Surveyor**
Chapman Land Surveying:
Bill Chapman
Harry Hickman

**General Contractor**
Hart Tipton Construction:
Jason Hart
Joelle Ciona
Glenn Thompson
Kensuke Yamamoto

**CONSTRUCTION COLLABORATORS & SUPPLIERS**

**Millwork & Interior Finishes**
Leon Leboniste:
Jon Hewitt
Grant Stacey
Andrew Campbell
Yasha Ashayeri

**Construction Managment**
Bildx Construction:
Jim Lennox

**Aluminum Cladding**
Panelex Industries:
Gregory Palamarz

**Pool Construction**
Alka Pools:
Rob Danieli
Robert Casanova

**Plumbing Fixtures**
Ambient Showroom:
Daniel Ilnitchi
Julia Ilintchi

**Window Coverings**
Arama Jillings
Final Touch Windows & Doors

**Glazing**
Atlas Meridian Glassworks Inc:
Carlos Müller
Jack de Bucy

**Windows**
Panoramah Windows & Doors:
Claudio Oliveira

**Door Hardware**
CMC Architectural Hardware:
Bevan Jefferies

**Garage Door**
Diamond Doors:
Tim Suderman

**Landscape Installation Contractor**
Botanica Design
Chris Hatty
Jacqui Harvey
Alan Makarewicz
Connor Aubrey

**Fire Protection Systems**
Fire Busters Inc:
Hynek Suda

**Lighting**
Perspective Lighting:
Lesley Ord

**Architectural Metal Work**
Drabek Technologies:
Martin Drabek

**Electrical**
Kuban Electric:
Toby Kuban
Doug Johnson

**Climatization**
Terra Mechanical:
John Rosse

**Elevators**
Western Elevator:
Cam Pomeroy

**Car Elevator & Car Lifts**
AC Lifts:
Brad Davies
Denis Pronin

**Stone Work**
NovaStone:
John Matas
Rees Fletcher

**Structural Steel**
Emsys: Jomel Bitoon

**Low Voltage / Automation**
Systems Audio Video:
Miles Morin

**Gas Fireplace**
Urban Fireplaces:
Dale Fouquette

**Suspended Fireplace**
CF+D Custom Fireplace Design:
Vince Volpe

**Custom Outdoor Furniture**
Barter Design Co:
Kenneth Torrance

**Midland Appliances**
Rob Davies

**Interior Furnishings**
Christian Woo (custom furniture)
Livingspace Interiors
Inform Interiors
Avenue Road

# PHOTOGRAPHY CAPTIONS

Covered terrace at sunset

 Descending the driveway towards the house. The glazed entrance allows for moments of reveal and anticipation during the approach.

 Looking west from upper floor "raised beach" landscape. The master bedroom is to the right.

 Waves at the beach

 View along drive toward courtyard and entry

 Entry approach from the courtyard garden

 View toward autocourt from entry

 Concrete flat work detail at entry

 Layers of reflection, solidity and transparency looking toward the water from the courtyard

 Towards the sky from lightwell

 Dark stained Accoya cladding and the reflections of board-formed concrete at the lightwell

 From entry to kitchen with reflections from the garden courtyard

 The office adjacent to kitchen opens to a deep lightwell and offers glimpses into the courtyard.

 Office from lightwell

 Dining room

 The dining room is defined by a millwork volume and connected directly to the kitchen.

Oak millwork in the kitchen and dining areas contrasts with cooler materials on the floor and ceiling.

 Seamless ceiling and floor treatments connect the kitchen to exterior covered areas.

 Underside of terrace cantilever showing water control details and wood soffit

 Detail of covered terrace from pool, sliding doors open

 Covered terrace provides framed views of water

 Living room

 View of main living space looking back toward courtyard

 Dining room

 Furnishings in the living room

 Gyrofocus fireplace at living room with custom hearth and furnishings

 Terrace from the east with overhanging pine trees

 The courtyard garden creates moments of natural connection and surprising reflections at the centre of the house.

 Oak lines the blackened steel structural stair

 The relationship between the stair and the exterior courtyard creates a moment of disorientation between in/out, up/down.

 Stair guardrail detail

 Stair detail

Stair and guardrail detail at entry

 Main level terrace from corner of pool

 View of the water from dining room

 Living room with views to pool and water

 Reflections play across glazing and still water

 Living and dining from pool

 Principal bedroom with "raised beach" landscape beyond

 Furnishing and material details at principal bedroom

 Highly customized closet at principal bedroom

 Corner glazing at principal bathroom with "raised beach" landscape beyond

 Principal bathroom with direct views to exterior landscape areas of the "upper beach"

 Upper level "beach" looking toward bedrooms with Arbutus tree

 Aluminum cladding detail at upper level

 Private terrace at guest suite

 Secondary bedrooms with direct access to the upper garden

 Looking south through the upper garden. The secondary bedrooms (to the left) all share this space.

Pool from lower garden. The building appears nestled in the landscape.

 Landscape at bottom of lightwell from guest bedroom

 Sauna

 Spa bathroom faucet detail

 Spa

 Spa nestled in landscape with views towards water

 The lifted edge of the pool is visually paired with the raised beach at the upper level.

 View towards spa and office

 "Board-form" concrete detail

 Outdoor Spa nestled in beachside meadow

 Expansive ocean views from upper patio

 Liminal house from the beach at low tide

 Path in lower garden

 *Arbutus x 'Marina'* along driveway slope

 Combination planting of *Erodium chamaedryoides* and *Sedum pachyclados* lines the driveway

 *Lavandula* and *Stipa* grass overhanging concrete wall

*Hippophae* and *Lavandula* provide texture against board-formed concrete

 Fruit of *Hippophae rhamnoides* appears in late summer

 Basalt cobbles provide transition between the plantings and the bedrooms

 *Eryngium giganteum*

 *Eryngium planum* 'Blaukappe'

 Mixed *Eryngium* planting

 Contrasting flower shapes in rooftop mixed meadow against concrete wall

 Hot pool at lower level

 *Erodium chamaedryoides* softens the basalt pathway

 Basalt step detail at corner of pool

 Path through beach garden

 Beachside meadow at lower level

 Informal pathway leads through matrix planting

 View of beachside planting from upper patio

 Lower garden seating forms a quiet alcove among landscape and architecture

 Basalt patio with soft seating

*Echinacea pallida* 'Hula dancer'

*Dianthus carthusianorum*, *Lavandula* 'Sawyers', and *Sanguisorba* 'Tootsee' on upper patio

Steel pickets allow perennials to grow without constraint on upper patio

*Pinus parviflora* frames the ocean view while obscuring the neighbouring property

A basalt pathway leads to an informal patio featuring a corten firebowl.

Large *Pinus* specimen reflected in the pool

Waves at the beach

# DESIGNERS

Photography by Goehring

**Matt Mcleod** and **Lisa Bovell** graduated in 2000 from the University of British Columbia with Masters of Architecture degrees. They formed a collaborative design partnership specializing in complete residential design in 2008. Since that time, Mcleod Bovell has grown to include a group of 17 designers with diverse backgrounds.

The studio works to understand the substantive elements of its client's desires and, through continuous dialog, establish frameworks for design-making. Ideas evolve from investigation rather than from pre-conceived or prescriptive solutions. Spatial experiences and idiosyncrasies are prioritized. Through these processes we create meaningful houses that convey feeling, specificity of character, and are receptive to influences beyond our region.

# BOOK CREDITS

Graphic design by Juan Sarrabayrouse
Art direction by Oscar Riera Ojeda
Copy editing by Kit Maude

**OSCAR RIERA OJEDA**
PUBLISHERS

Copyright © 2024 by Oscar Riera Ojeda Publishers Limited
ISBN 978-1-964490-02-1
Published by Oscar Riera Ojeda Publishers Limited
Printed in China

Oscar Riera Ojeda Publishers Limited
Unit 1331, Beverley Commercial Centre,
87-105 Chatham Road South, Tsim Sha Tsui, Kowloon, Hong Kong

Production Offices
Suit 19, Shenyun Road,
Nanshan District, Shenzhen 518055, China

International Customer Service & Editorial Questions: +1-484-502-5400

www.oropublishers.com | www.oscarrieraojeda.com
oscar@oscarrieraojeda.com

All rights reserved. No part of this book may be reproduced, stored in a retrieval system, or transmitted in any form or by any means, including electronic, mechanical, photocopying or microfilming, recording, or otherwise (except that copying permitted by Sections 107 and 108 of the U.S. Copyright Law and except by reviewers for the public press) without written permission from the publisher.